What's Your Story?

ANNIKA SPALDING

It's your time to shine!
Love Annika Spald
x

Visit the author's website at **www.annikaspalding.co.uk**

Cover designed by Gavin Telfer

ISBN-10: 1973722631
ISBN-13: 978-1973722632

To every aspiring writer who thinks they can't reach their writing
goal...
Plot twist: You can.

Annika Spalding

CONTENTS

Annika Spalding

ACKNOWLEDGEMENTS

I'd like to thank my growing list of supporters who encourage me to keep writing. Every word in this book has been written with you in mind.

My children, Amelia and Mya, for reminding me constantly why I put so much faith in my writing and the work that I do. This legacy I am building is for them.

I'd like to thank my accountability buddy, mentor and friend Paula Hemmings for keeping me on task. You believed in my vision and reminded me of my potential at times when I dwindled.

I'd like to thank my editor and friend Jordan Garvey for being a trusted pair of second eyes. You're the only person in my immediate circle who understands writing like I do, and that has stopped this from being a lonely journey.

My friends and family who avoid asking me, "How's that book coming along?" because they know nobody needs that kind of pressure.

My followers on social media and in real life, thank you for believing in me. The strength of that belief has been motivation enough for me to finish this book.

This is for you.

What's Your Story?

If you were a book, what would your title be? Would your cover design catch my eye or would you blend in with the surroundings? Would the blurb invite me to read the content? They say you shouldn't judge a book by its cover, but have you been taking care of yours? Are your corners damaged, pages torn, jacket defaced with graffiti? Have you been read to death or are you collecting dust on the shelf?

I was on the shelf. I put myself there. In the dark; unseen and unheard. Collecting dust. It was lonely but it was comfortable. Life didn't seem to expect much of me and I didn't expect too much of it either. But in doing so I forgot about my value, I didn't recognise how my experiences are fuel for stories that could inspire others. I forgot about my own point of view, the words of wisdom acquired over the years and overlooked my true value. I lost my self-worth and nobody helped me look for it.

But I was full of ideas. I used to be a person of great ideas but failed to make it happen. All talk and no action. You've heard of that, right? That was me. And I'm guessing that might have been you too.

A few years ago, I realised I had to do something with my ideas. I decided that I was here for a purpose greater than what I knew and a magical feeling overwhelmed me, so great that I had to do something with it. I surrendered to it, curious about where it might take me.

This magic demanded I let go of all relationships that didn't enhance my life in any way. I let them go. This magic demanded that I finish the book I was writing, that I trust in the story and complete that journey. I did it. This magic demanded I try something new, go to a creative evening and mingle with different people. I did it. This magic convinced me that I was beyond capable of building the life I deserved, beyond capable to ensure my children have a great childhood. This magic told me to listen, even when there were no clear steps to take, I had to try moving forward anyway.

This magic was powerful. Before I knew it, I was changing and so was my life. It had inspired growth and that was scary, but this magic told me to trust myself. So, I did.

And here I am, award winning author, writing coach, mature student, beginning again as a single mum with a dream, and all because I trusted magic, something I couldn't see: a gentle nudge inside that whispered "self-belief".

Now it's time to give back, if you're listening to me now, I want to encourage you to go forward and listen to your own magic.

It's time to stop re-reading the painful chapters of your life. It's time to let the past go. Turn the page, close the book and start again because you are the author of your story and you get to decide what happens from here.

It's time to step out of the shadows, off the shelf and into the light. Into your greatness. It's your time to shine. Your life may not have turned out how you planned or expected but it is yours! Take back your power, stop trying to fit in, change direction! It's time to stand up and be noticed.

Bring a new voice, a new narrative, a new outlook, a new energy to your story. Redesign the cover. Give yourself a new title. Call back the old copies of you because although valuable, they no longer represent you.

You are no longer a victim of life circumstances, you are a survivor and you can move forward as a life enthusiast. Trust the magic inside that tells you that you are destined for greatness. You have so much to give to the world if only you would take the time to take better care of yourself.

Don't leave yourself on the shelf. Demand to be read.

Now tell me, what's your new story?

What This Book Will Do for You

Initially this book was created as an online course because I wanted to encourage people to dig deep and write their truth. But I wasn't 100% sure about putting it out there in that format, it didn't quite feel right.

I took the time to think about what I could do with all the work I had produced and worked out an alternative plan that would ensure my supporters benefit from my efforts. And here we are.

The intention is that this book will get you writing. You'll be inspired by the content of the pages, and find yourself a willing participant in the exercises. You'll be overcome with a feeling that you might not recognise, simply because you've tried something new. And I'm hoping, really hoping that by the time you reach the end you'll be proud of what you have achieved.

Writing can be challenging even for experienced writers, and if you're just starting out on your writing journey it can be overwhelmingly daunting. Over the years I have spoken to many people who have the most amazing ideas for books, yet they fail to launch their idea off the ground. I became a writing coach because I understood how important it is to address our internal blockages in order to let our creativity flow. I became a writing coach because I understand how accountability and guidance can enhance a writer's experience, especially when they're writing a book.

What often appears as an impossible mountain to climb, can certainly be broken down into manageable hikes, and this is the approach I like to bring to writing. How can you write a book if the very idea of writing anything seems daunting?

I want you to express yourself in a way you haven't before. I want to provide you with the opportunity to dig deep and address how you feel about life experiences. I want you to write more than you expected to, about things you've never dared speak about. I want you to rediscover and feel inspired and moved by something you're written, because I want you to realise how powerful your words can be.

This book will not teach you linguistics or the rules of grammar and punctuation. It will not demand hours and hours of your time to work through it all at once, a little at a time will be enough. This book will not solve your problems, it will not pay your bills or grant you five years of youth, but it has the power to change your life.

It has the power to change your life, if you're open to the possibility. If you participate. If you try.

It has the power to help you find and connect with your authentic writing voice and encourage you to write without fear.

This book has the power to draw you out of your comfort zone, if you're willing to let it go.

If you're willing to let go of the idea that you can't write and that nobody would read it if you did. Know that this notion simply isn't true.

If you're willing to consider the possibility that your words matter, that you can write and surprise yourself with the results of your efforts, then this is the right book for you.

If you're reading this book you are ready, ready to take a step away from fear, so that you can move closer to writing the story you've been holding onto all this time.

Welcome.

Part One: Self-Acceptance

Are You Selling Yourself Short?

We are the first to criticise ourselves and the last to leave a compliment.

From a young age, we are conditioned to believe that we are not enough. We learn the importance of fitting in and being accepted, and in the process, lose our sense of individuality.

Comfort is found in doing what everybody else is doing but I will tell you now there is no growth in the comfort zone. If you only place value in what other people say about you, you'll never find that peace within yourself. You'll never find value in what you say.

Your voice is important.

Let's assume we're already starting at a point where you don't appreciate the person you are. You find it difficult to accept compliments and you crave approval from your peers to validate who you are. It's not a great position to be in but so many of us are. You are not alone.

We are so used to thinking about what is wrong with us that we don't even see all that is right with us. But I assure you, there is so much right with you, you simply haven't been given the space to see it yet, so let's unpack it together.

In the box on the following page, write ten of your strongest qualities.

```
1.

2.

3.

4.

5.

6.

7.

8.

9.

10.
```

How was that? Easy? A challenge?

So, let's try something else.
Imagine you are temporarily in the mind of someone who is close
to you.

- How do they view you?
- How do you make them feel?
- What would they say are your flaws and your strengths?
- Are you a good friend?

    If you were a book, how would they write a review of your
    content?

Write in the space below and include the points on the previous page.

It is easier for us to view ourselves positively through the eyes of another.

You have so much to offer, but fail to see this in the same way the world does. If you're somebody who is destined for greatness (the fact that you're even reading this suggests that you are), then you must know your voice, your knowledge, your skills have value, and you can take these steps to achieve your goals, writing or otherwise.

This is not going to happen overnight, changing your mindset from "I can't" to "I can" takes time. But you can do this. It's time to stop underestimating yourself. It's time to step into your greatness and accept yourself for the strong, resilient person that you have always been, even if you don't see it yet.

Significant Events

If we are to move forward and be happy in life, we must first address and make peace with the past.

As much as we assume we have overcome incidents and upheavals, the impact of significant events stay with us much longer than we realise.

If you are committed to loving yourself, you must forgive yourself. You must be kinder to the person that you are, because you would not be here today if it wasn't for the person that you once were.

You must acknowledge that you aren't perfect, nobody is, because perfection does not exist, so why strive for it?

All you can be is better than the person you were yesterday. The person yesterday had to experience significant events to be the person you are today, and that is what we'll look at next.

What is a significant event?

A significant event is a point of reference, when something happened that had an impact on you and remains engraved in your memory. Your experience of this shapes your views, moulds your emotions, alters your expectations and at times becomes a turning point for change.

Significant events can be different for everybody and affect people in all sorts of ways, if at all. Right now, we're focusing on you and your life up until this point.

What has led you here? Was it a decision in response to an incident outside of your control? How do you cope with the aftermath? It's a lot to consider all at once, but it is important to appreciate where you are in your journey. But how can you do that if you don't even acknowledge what you've been faced with and have overcome?

Let's look at the significant events in your life.
Fill in the gaps. Be honest, nobody should read this but you.

Age	Significant event	How did you feel then?	How do you feel about it now?
0-5yrs			
6-11yrs			
12-17yrs			
18-23yrs			
24-29yrs			

30-35yrs			
36-41yrs			
42-47yrs			
48+			

Now take a moment. In fact, put this sheet away for an hour. Have a tea break, make lunch, listen to music, switch off for an hour at least. Take a whole day if you need to. Have a break.

Why?

It's good to take time to process the information your pour out. It is likely you remembered things you'd forgotten. It is likely that during your break you will remember a few more, you can add them on your return.

It is likely at this moment; you don't yet understand the enormity of what your life was and what you've been through.

Back from your break?
Read through what you've written on the previous page. In fact, read it out loud. If you can, stand in front of a mirror. Look at the

person looking back at you and make eye contact. When you're ready, read what you've written to your reflection. Start your sentences with "When you were three, this happened, it made you feel, and now you feel…" etc.

It's one thing for a memory to stay lodged in our minds, quite another to dig it out and write it down. Feel the conviction in your voice as you speak. Listen to the words that come out of your mouth as you read what you've written. That is your truth and this is important.

What did this exercise teach you about your past?

How does it feel to see your life written out?

What about this task was hard?

Why?

What about this task was easy?

Why?

What have you learned about yourself?

Why?

Do you see how powerful your words are? When you write your experiences down and read them back, it made you feel something. It made you connect with the reality of what you have been through, rather than it being tucked away at the back of your mind.

These significant events matter because they had an impact on you. To leave the past behind, we must take ownership of it. You can't change it; nor can you hide from it because it is part of who you are.

But it doesn't have to define who you are.

What's Your Story?

Have you completed the Significant Events worksheet? Awesome. Now let's focus on your story.

There are two types of people. There are those who live life and there are those who simply exist.

I'll tell you a secret: **you are here to do more than just exist.** Who you are, the life you've lived up until this point and the plans you have for the future, all of it is important. The experiences that shaped you, the feelings you had in response to them, none of it was in vain. It's part of your life and that's what brought you here in the first place.

What do we know about stories?
As a minimum, they mostly have a beginning, middle and end. We know they have a title that is engaging but doesn't give too much away about the plot. There will be a main character who'll be the protagonist, another character who is the antagonist, and a bunch of secondary characters that don't matter as much as the main. Add a dash of conflict and we have a story.

Let's get started.
Using the Significant Events worksheet, complete the details on the following page.

What was your beginning?

What was your middle?

What will your end look like?

What have been the common themes?

Who is the protagonist?

Who is the antagonist?

What would you title your story?

If you could change anything, what would it be and why?

Think of your life as a story and you are the author.

It belongs to you. It is yours, the good bits and the bad. There are parts that appear ugly or painful, then there are those which warm your heart and make you smile. A good book has balance of the good and the bad, and your life is no different.

Know that you are the author of the next chapter.
You get a say in how you move forward. You don't have to repeat the mistakes you made in the past, you can choose differently this time. And know that despite any sense of self-doubt you may feel today, you have overcome so much already. Read it back until you digest it.

If you can get through the highs and lows of your beginnings and middles, then you're well equipped to continue with wisdom right until the end.

Dear Inner Child

You've paid attention to your past, listed the events, given time to think about the impact, summarised your story and now it's time to heal.

Entertain this: your inner child is sat on a chair opposite you.

Think about: What do they look like? What are they wearing? Are they sitting upright with confidence or are they hunched up and timid? What do they need right now?

Write: On the next page, write a letter of love and encouragement to your Inner Child. Soothe them. Comfort them. Assure them that everything will be okay and tell them what makes you so sure of that.

Remember: You are the adult.

Feeling brave? Post it to the *Writing With Confidence* group.

Dear Inner Child,

Part Two: Self Discovery

What's Your Why?

When setting any goal, it's important to know exactly what is motivating us to working towards them. But before we do that, let's look at your life right now.

Using the mind map template below, write down your entire life as it stands at present. Include your many roles and responsibilities, what you do and who you take care of.

Now you've written it all out, answer the following questions:

How does it feel to see your current life written out?

What do you want to change and why?

How do you think you'd feel if you made those changes?

If you could pick three areas of improvement to work on, what would they be?

Why are they important?

Let's try something else. Imagine you've implemented those changes and your life has dramatically improved.

In the space below, complete the mind map as though you are at that point of improvement and benefiting from it.

What would it look like? What would your roles and responsibilities be?

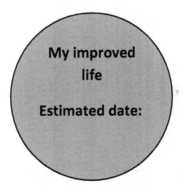

Now you've written it all out, answer the following questions:

How does it feel to see your future life written out?

What changes have been most important and why?

Has anything you've written surprised you? Why?

Are you ready to take the next step?

It is not unusual for people to say they want to write a book but take very little action to get there.

To write a book, or blog, or script, or anything of great length, means to commit to your craft. It means to create space in your day to work on your writing and to persevere against any negative thoughts or outside influences.

It sounds complicated enough, but at this point of the course you've already been writing away. The exercises have been designed to distract you from the practice and focus on building the content, while also giving you a feel for writing.

Let's take action!

Working on ourselves requires daily effort. From self-love to confidence in writing, whatever we focus on, to fully benefit from the investment of our time we have to work on it every day.

Look at the goals you set out on the last page.

Don't be distracted by huge steps, think about the small things you can do each day to bring you closer to your goals.

Keep in mind:
There's no point having a goal but not working towards it. There's no point having tasks so big that you don't even try.

Dedicating even 30 minutes each day to doing better will leave you feeling better than you would if you hadn't made time.

As you're reading this book, I'm hoping you are clear about why you want to develop your confidence about writing.

To reflect that, use the table on the next page to create an action plan. You may want to refer to the previous sheet for inspiration. I have included an example of my own that you may wish to try.

What I want to achieve.	Why?	How it will feel to achieve this.	What I am prepared to do to get there.
Develop a healthy writing habit.	Because I want to write a book.	Amazing!	Write in my journal every day.

Feel free to continue this in your own writing book, journal, or as a rough guide to create your own action plan.

The Importance of Accountability in Self-Love

To appreciate and value ourselves in any present moment means we have understood our lives up until that point.

The exercises you have completed so far should have helped you to look at and accept the significant events that you have overcome, which will lead you to discover who you are underneath it all. **YOU ARE STRONGER THAN YOU REALISE.**

You are worthy of your love, but to move forward with self-love you must let go of any negativity attached to the events that shaped the person you are today.

Like writing, self-love is a solitary journey but it doesn't have to be a lonely experience. Being open about being a work-in-progress enables you to find people who are also in the healing process too.

Sharing your goals with others means you are responsible for achieving them. Putting them into a public space means you will benefit from peer support, and this will encourage you to keep going.

In the *Writing With Confidence* Facebook group, post what you're going to do each day to bring you closer to self-love. Start with: "Today/This week I'm going to… because it will make me feel…"

You're worth the time and energy you will invest in yourself to complete what you set out to do.

Dear Inner Child – Part 2

You've written a letter of love and encouragement to your inner child, now it's time to give thanks.

It could be said that our inner child is working hard to keep us safe, represented as fear. But often when fear steps in, we allow it to stop us from taking risks or trying something new. Instead of fighting against it, it's time to acknowledge its existence because it is part of the human experience. It is part of you.

Entertain this: your inner child has been acting out of fear to protect you from harm all these years.

Think about: Your inner child feels responsible for your safety, why? How tiring is it for them to be on constant-alert? How must it feel to be scared all the time?

Write: On the next page, write a letter of thanks to your Inner Child. Acknowledge their efforts in keeping you safe.

Remember: You don't have to share this with anyone, if you don't want to. Write as if nobody will ever read it, so that your true thoughts pour out and your authenticity shows.

Be brave: Post it to the *Writing With Confidence* Facebook group.

Dear Inner Child…

Part Three: Discovering Writing

5 Day Writing Challenge

Think of writing as a muscle; it needs daily exercise to get stronger. Commit to a fixed work-out schedule, and you'll most certainly feel the benefits! If you want to write a book, blog or write generally with confidence, you must work on it every day.

The 5 Day Writing Challenge gives you the opportunity to get yourself into a writing mindset. As it is for only five days, it is short enough for you to avoid feeling overwhelmed, but also long enough for you to get a sense of what it means to write daily.

This challenge will show you exactly what you can achieve, if you have a plan and commit to it.

- Set yourself a daily minimum word count. I'd say 200 words is a good place to start. (You can increase it every time.)
- Set your own writing theme for each day or use the prompts on the following page as a guide.
- Where do you like to write? Whether it's your phone, your writing book, your laptop or tablet, maybe a mixture of them all, be prepared to write a minimum of 200 words.
- Start today! Don't wait for Monday, just do it!

Feeling brave? Share what you've written for the 5 Day Writing Challenge on the *Writing With Confidence* Facebook group!

Prompts

Pick a prompt at random and then write about it!

My childhood dream	Lunchtime musings	Adventure
My favourite film	My relationship with my mother	Dear Negative Self-Talk
Five things I love about the internet	Ego	My morning routine
A promise I broke	The person I was versus the person I am	My favourite place
The day I missed lunch	Forgiveness	We don't speak anymore but...
Patience	Chocolate cake	The last time I laughed
Why I deserved that bubble bath	Unleashing the real me	All the reasons why I am not a horrible person
Taking chances	Self-Love	Where I see myself in 5 years
Ghosts exist and this is how I know	Write the job description for parenthood	The sound of rain in the morning
A conversation I heard on the bus	What I'd say to the me from 5 years ago	Why I'm letting the past go

The Benefits of Journaling

To some it is a diary, to others it's a journal, either way there is more than one way to write.

To find your writing voice, you must give yourself the opportunity to express yourself in a safe environment. When you journal, nobody else should read it to give you the space to be honest. This will give you a sense of freedom, because the rules of society don't apply when you write only for your eyes.

If you're a person with their guard up, journaling allows you to see what you've been thinking, unedited and unheard. It allows you to express your thoughts and feelings in a way you might not have done otherwise.

Sometimes, we don't quite realise what we're thinking until we read it back.

Journaling is a good way to document the turning points of our life, the decisions we make and how we feel about them, enabling us to reflect on our highs and lows. It is a great tool to measure our growth.

Some people write notes in their phones, some keep a writing book, try both and see what works for you.

Five points to remember
Who: Write as if nobody will ever read it. Write for you.
What: Write down your thoughts and experiences. Summarise

your day.

How: It doesn't have to be complicated. It doesn't have to be perfect. It just must be from you.

Where: Use a laptop, PC, tablet, phone, notebook or whatever else you can find. Keep all your journal entries in one place.

Why: To give yourself an outlet.

Best time of day?

Experiment. Try the first ten minutes of your day before you've rolled out of bed. See how it feels to write at lunchtime. Or perhaps it works best to write out your thoughts before you go to sleep. There is no wrong time of day, all writers have different preferences, so go with what feels good for you.

REMEMBER

We all have time to write. It is a choice we make. You could write a few bullet points while you wait for your bath to run, or while the kettle boils, sitting in the doctor's waiting room or when you're enjoying your Sunday morning lie in. Use that time to write!

The Benefits of Blogging

Blogging is a wonderful way to take your writing to the public. Blogging has become a phenomenon. A unique way of showcasing your knowledge and passions, and attracting readers from all over the globe.

It is very simple:
Identify something you know a lot about and write about it. Popular topics range from hair and beauty, parenting, mental illness, writing tips and much more.

You don't need to have a degree in Creative Writing to develop a blog with a strong following. You don't even need to be an IT expert.

All you need to do, before you do anything else, is write.

Think of it as an online journal.
You can connect with other people through your writing, on many different topics (and by sharing at your discretion).
People utilise this platform to establish themselves and their ideas. Your ideas and experiences can be presented uniquely, and you are in control of that.
It's a great way to know that you are not alone in your thinking and that someone relates to your experiences or is as enthusiastic about issues as you are.

Five points to remember
Who: You can write for yourself but the topics you cover can be influenced by the feedback from your readers.

What: Literally *anything*. Life experiences, study tips, cooking recipes, book reviews, it's entirely up to you.

How: Use an online blogging platform. Make notes on what you'd like to write about, type up, edit and go!

Where: Anywhere you can access the internet from.

Why: To tell your story, create a following, gain feedback, connect with people and explore writing themes.

Best time of day?

Blogging platforms collect data which will tell you which times of day to post. You can write your notes at any time but be mindful to post at a time that your following is most active. The only way to figure that out is to try it!

REMEMBER

You already have blogging content, you must identify what it is, write about it and share it with the world.

Reading Research

A good writer is passionate about the art of the written word.
If you're aspiring to write, whether it is a blog or book, it is
important to understand how to get your readers attention.

Make use of your reading collection and Google to complete the
table below.

Books/blogs you've read			
What makes it good/bad?			
What caught your eye?			
How did it make you feel?			
Would you recommend it? Why?			

What Writers Fear

To be a writer is to accept vulnerability, because putting your precious work in a public sphere is potentially terrifying.
It is natural to fear rejection, especially with something you have spent time creating and perfecting. To be knocked back and have your work overlooked or criticised, is enough to diminish any trace of confidence you have as a writer. But when this happens, you have two choices: 1. Carry on or, 2. Quit. (Here's a secret: Good writers don't quit.)

To be a writer requires a level of discipline.
The activity of writing is reliant upon mindset: you must do it more than you think of it. Yet, we create excuses because it simply is not easy to write. There are those who wait for a moment of inspiration before they put pen to paper. But then there are others who are committed to the craft and dedicate time to writing long after the feeling has passed. Which one are you?

If fear is part of a mindset, then it can be challenged and overcome. It is a temporary state of mind, not a permanent one, and the moment you realise this, you'll defeat writer's block and finish what you started.

Fear	Why	How to Overcome It.
Rejection	"People will hate my writing"	Understand that not everyone will love what you do. Just as you don't like everything, your writing will appeal to a select few, and that is okay. An audience that is specific is easier to cater for and market at.
Mediocracy	"My writing isn't up to standard."	As a writer, you're going to be very self-critical. Nobody wakes up a flawless writer, it takes time and practice to write well. Take responsibility for your improvement. Read books about writing. Sign up to creative writing courses and attend workshops. Self-study; the world is your oyster. Try new genres. Push yourself to learn more than what you already know, and apply that to your knowledge. Test new work on your audience and use that criticism to direct your growth.

Misunderstood	"My message will be lost."	Be clear about your message, to yourself before you write for anyone else. Carefully select your words to convey that message in a way that leaves you satisfied. Understand that a good writer isn't necessarily the one who writes the most. A good writer is one who can say twice as much with half the amount of words.
Procrastination	"I can't do this so I'm not even going to try."	We can be our own enemies but it is a choice. We all have the same hours in each day but it is how we choose to spend that time that separates us. If you want to reach your writing goals, you must choose action over inactivity. Push yourself out of the comfort zone and write your word limit each day.

Allowing fear to stop you from writing is an injustice to your creativity. Feel the fear, embrace it, take it and write anyway

Part Four: Documenting Your Journey

Congratulations! You're a writer!

Read the title of this chapter again. YOU ARE A WRITER!

Convinced? Yeah, I didn't think so. Read on.

Welcome to Part Four! If you have read the book in order, you would have completed various exercises and takes to get to this point. By design, the different exercises are thought-provoking and created to encourage you to place more focus on creating content than the fact you're writing.

A dreamer dreams but a writer writes, and so by regularly putting pen to paper you have become a writer. You have completed the takes, produced written work, so how could you be anything else?

Knowing you are a writer is half the journey, but doing something about it can feel like an uphill hike.

Hopefully at this point you would have found a preferred medium and a time of day to write, and are beginning to understand what kind of writer you are. Remember, you define your identity and experience.

In your mind, what makes a writer a writer? And what makes you a writer? Understand there are no two writers who are exactly like the same. You mustn't compare your level of creativity to another's, because if you are writing then you can claim the title of a writer as your own.

Of course, there are those who are dedicated to the craft, but even they began somewhere. They were once where you are now.

Reflection & Growth

To move forward with wisdom, it is necessary to reflect on what we have learned so far.

Complete the questions below with honesty to get the most out of this experience.

Describe your writing habits before you read this book:	
Describe your writing habits now:	
What did the Inner Child activities teach you?	
What was an unexpected lesson and why?	
What do you understand now that you didn't before?	
How did you find the 5 Day Writing Challenge?	

What did the 5 Day Writing Challenge teach you?	
What have you learned about yourself so far?	
How do you plan to implement what you have learned so far?	
What kind of writer were you?	
What kind of writer would you like to be?	
How ready are you to move forward with your writing?	

Feeling brave? Post one or two answers in the *Writing With Confidence* Facebook group.

Powerful Words

Understand this: words have power.
They provoke reactions and emotions we never knew existed.
Powerful words invite us to feel, reflect, assess and grow.
Used negatively, words can wound us and bring us to a dark place.
Knowing this means we have great responsibility in how we put words together.
Get it wrong and your message will be lost.
Get it right and you'll make a positive impact that ripples long after the moment of creation.

Affirmations are positive statements created to reinforce positive beliefs.
Rather than looking externally for approval, affirmations encourage you to see validation from yourself through the power of words.
To experience the power of words, try applying them to your daily routine. You could write them on post-its and stick them to your mirror, repeat them out loud before you get out of bed, and write them down in a moment of anxiety.
Here's a few to get you started. Feel free to add a few of your own.

- I am a strong and powerful being.
- I am a force to be reckoned with.
- I am happy on purpose.
- I am capable of anything.
- I am a good writer.
- My writing has value.
- I will change lives with my words.
- I will finish writing my book and I will take the next step.
-

-
-
-
-
-
-
-
-
-
-
-
-
-
-
-
-
-
-

These statements should be said with conviction and leave no room for doubt. They should be repeated until you feel the effects.

Feeling brave? Share your affirmations in the *Writing With Confidence* Facebook group!

Private Vs Public

It can't be avoided; criticism shapes our writing. But it isn't always a bad thing.

There are many benefits to writing for yourself and for the public. While writing for the public can seem like a risky option, writing for yourself offers a sense of security and protection from hurtful words.

But how can you truly know whether your writing is of a good standard if you've never let anyone else read it?

Family and friends may not necessarily give you the feedback you need to grow as a writer, but the public is unbiased and often unedited in its view of your work.

To put your work out into a public space means you must develop thick skin and be prepared for all sorts of feedback.

While the compliments can boost your confidence, the criticism can help shape your focus and identify areas that may need additional nurturing.

Weigh up the pros and cons.

Maybe begin with writing for yourself, stick to your journal or the notes app in your phone, until you get used to writing regularly.

But also, consider the next step, sharing your written words with a wider audience.

But before you venture out, here's some food for thought on the following page:

	Pros	Cons
Private	• You can express yourself freely without external judgement • You can explore different types of writing • You can analyse yourself through what you write • It is therapeutic • There is no consequence for expressing a controversial opinion or idea	• You don't know how people will react to your writing as only you see it • You don't know how good you are or where you might need to learn more • You talk yourself out of sharing any of your writing and remain in the comfort zone

Public	• You can connect with other people through your writing • You can utilise it as a tool for creating a business/brand following • You can monetise it • It can prompt other opportunities e.g. public speaking	• You must be able to withstand a variety of criticisms • Your words may be misinterpreted • Everything you write is documented and accessed by all • You must develop a thick skin as initially some criticisms will hurt

Complete the following:

Your reasons for writing for yourself:

Your reasons for writing for the public:

Feeling brave? Share what you've written Challenge in the *Writing With Confidence* Facebook page!

Part Five: Moving Forward

Moving Forward – Blogging

It's time to take your ideas to a blogging platform!
You have strong ideas and want to test it with a virtual audience, blogging is a free and quick way to do that.
But rather than dive in head first, it's well worth planning your blog before you set it up.

It is recommended that you look at the different blogging platforms before you decide which one to use.
A popular site is Wordpress.com, and this also has a downloadable app so that you can update your blog directly from your phone. But there are others, which include Blogger, Weebly and Tumblr, to name a few.

What is already out there?
Take time to look through the blogging communities. Just a quick Google search will give you results to start sifting through. Take note of the different layouts and images used. Find out how often these bloggers post content. Look for blogs that are likely to be similar to yours.

Some things to consider:
- What would you write about? Start with a topic of interest.
- What would you call it? Make it memorable.
- Would you write under your own name or create a pseudonym? Consider that people like to connect with people.
- How often would you like to blog? It could be weekly, fortnightly or monthly, whatever works for you. Just be consistent.

Challenge:
- Use the notes above to plan for your blog.
- Head on over to WordPress and follow the steps to create a free blog.
- Write a blog post about how you feel about starting a blog.
- Post the link to the *Writing With Confidence* Facebook group.
- Remember, it doesn't have to be perfect, this is just to get you started.

Keep all your information in one place.
Use the table below to guide you.

My blog is called	
The web address is	
The topics I will cover are	
I write under the name	
I plan to blog every	Week/Fortnight/Month/Whenever I feel like it
My target audience is	

Feeling brave? Share your blog details in the *Writing With Confidence* Facebook group!

FAQ About Blogging

As with anything you're unfamiliar with, blogging can seem complicated – but it doesn't have to be.

You'll find step-by-step instructions on each blogging platform on how to set up a blog, but it is often the bit that comes afterwards that is more of a challenge. Not only do you have to create content, you are also responsible for promoting your blog, networking with other bloggers and seeking opportunities to grow your community.

Everybody has a starting point and this is just yours. You'll learn things along the way that will help you and will shape your experience of what it means to be a blogger.

Here are some FAQ to help dispel any worries or concerns you may have.

1. What if my idea isn't unique?
It is likely that someone else has had an idea like yours, but don't let that deter you. What you must keep in mind is that you offer a unique perspective and you also have your own writing style.

Embrace your individuality because this is what will make you stand out the most, especially if it comes across in your writing.

2. Should I use images?
Images are a great way to make text visually appealing, especially if they are relevant to what has been written. So, in short, absolutely.

3. Where should I get my images from?

Photos we find floating around on the internet aren't necessarily free. There's nothing worse than using a photo from Google and then being contacted by the owner because you used it without permission.

To avoid being sued, it is recommended you use images you take yourself or free stock photos available on various sites on the internet.

If you take them yourself, you don't need to have a professional camera, even a camera on a mobile phone can produce good quality photos. Experiment with different angles, lighting and colours.

If you use free stock photos, double check whether you need to credit the image owner when you use them.

4. How long should my posts be?

This is entirely up to you and depends on the kind of post you are writing. Ideally, it would be awesome to have something longer than a Tweet but shorter than a book. Maybe start with around 500 -1000 words, keeping in mind that use of images also helps to break up the text.

A long blog post doesn't guarantee a good read, so focus instead on making the content interesting enough for your audience to read until the end.

5. Can I swear in blog posts?

Absolutely! It's your blog, right? The thing with writing is that we can write what we want. Not everybody enjoys profanity but others love to use it to express themselves.

Top tip: Swearing in your text should enhance the meaning rather than take attention away from the message you are trying to convey. Less is more, and if it fits the tone then go ahead. But you are a writer and there are different words you can use to express that you are annoyed, frustrated, in a state of upset or simply pissed off. See what I did there?

6.   How do I connect with other bloggers?

Blogging works the way that it does now through the power of networking. Make use of Facebook groups, Twitter networking hours and attend blogging events. Remember, if you don't talk about your blog, how will anyone know about it?

7.   How can I get people to read my blog?

Promote it via WhatsApp, social media, send it via email to your contacts, talk about it with your friends, comment on other blogs and generally put yourself out there. There are people who will stumble across your blog by accident, but you can help reach an audience by promoting yourself too.

8.   Should I write under my own name?

People like to connect with people and this means it helps to write under your own name when you blog. However, depending on the type of content, you may opt for a pseudonym to protect your identity. You can share as much or as little as you like.

9.   How can I check to see how many readers I have?

Blogging platforms like WordPress collect information about who reads your blog posts, what country they are from; how they find your blog, etc. This is a great way to understand your audience and it may bring you surprises too. These statistics also show you which blog post was most popular, which is awesome when you're writing about different topics as this will indicate to you what your audience likes to read about.

10. When is the best time to post?

Using the statistics mentioned in the previous point, you will find out when your readers are online. Do not assume that your audience will be from your country, blogging reaches people from all over the world, which means different time zones.

You can blog at any time, the real skill is knowing when to share it on Facebook, Instagram and Twitter. But if you are serious about blogging and have set up business or professional pages for social media, you will be able to access this information too.

Moving Forward – Write a book

It's time to write a book! Or at least plan for it.
If you've ever wanted to write a book or at least toyed with the idea, then now is a great time to put it into action.

Writing a book can seem like a daunting task, and it is mostly. It isn't easy but with a good plan to guide you, you'll stay on track and reach your writing goal.

Some things to consider:
- **What kind of book will you write?** Will it be a collection of poetry, or a self-help guide? Perhaps you're a budding novelist, or maybe instead you want to write about business. Being clear about your vision is important because you must understand what it is you're writing about. If you don't understand, how will your readers?

- **What is the title?** Some authors have a title immediately; others wait until they've finished the book. Either way, have something that will do your work justice. Keep it simple but effective, if you choose to publish your work a strong title will be easy to use in marketing campaigns that use hashtags.

- **Research word count.** We're in an era of self-publishing but that doesn't mean you don't have to stick to the rules of writing. Word count is important and it is worth researching how many words make a novel etc. To know this in advance will help with your planning. It is important to have a milestone to work towards, at least as a guide while you write.

- **Plan your content!** Having a clear structure for your book will help with the completion process. How will you know you're done if you don't know if you have covered all the important points? I recommend you create a book plan following the Significant Events as a template. Use that to identify your main chapters or sections of your book, and then make key points under each of them.

- **Plan a writing schedule.** Your book won't write itself, it needs you and your dedicated time. Set aside time each day or week dedicated to writing. If you've planned your book, you'll be able to make the most of any time you have, whether it is an hour, half day or full day.

- **Research adds value**. Don't be afraid to dig deep for information you don't already know. This helps shape our writing and gives our audience the impression that we have put a lot of thought into our work. Apply wherever you feel is relevant.

- **Final note:** Write without fear and edit at the end.

Challenge:
- Write a thorough plan for your book, using everything you have learned.

Keep all your information in one place.
Use the table below to guide you.

What do you want to write about? List your different ideas.	
What are your three favourite ideas?	1. 2. 3.
Which would require the most research?	
Which would you like to read? *Write that.*	
What is your book called?	
Describe it in one sentence.	
Describe it in one paragraph.	
What genre is it?	
What are the main themes?	
What research is needed to complete this book?	

What word count are you working towards?	Weekly/Fortnightly/Monthly/Whenever I feel like it
Who is your target audience?	

The Story Flow

Writing a story, how hard can it be, right?

Basic stories have a beginning, middle and end. To make it more interesting, it is important to have a plot which involves some form of conflict. The meat of your story should be about battling and overcoming that conflict, to reach a satisfying conclusion.

Why is this important?

Well, you want your story to be interesting and make sense to the reader. How awful would it be to write something that people never finished reading because it bored them or confused them completely? Following a simple procedure will ensure that your story has enough highs and lows to keep the reader intrigued until the very end.

Here's a simple plan to get you started.

What is the name of your story?	
Overview of the story	
Describe the protagonist	
Describe the antagonist	

How does it begin?	
What goes wrong?	
What happens in the middle?	
What is at risk?	
Who saves the day?	
How does it end?	

Challenge:
- Write a short story of around 1000 words using your plan.

Feeling brave? Share your story in the *Writing With Confidence* Facebook group!

Writing Ideas

You can write about anything you like, which is exciting and scary all at the same time.

But don't let that stop you. It is not at all unusual to explore different types of writing before you decide which one is best suited for you. This is the same for the types of topics we write about.

To help prompt you, here are some topics you can write about for your blog, book or journal.

Diary of a Single Mother	Writing Tips for Beginners	Five Steps to Positivity	Cooking for the Family: 30 Minute Recipes
Knock Knock and Other Amazing Jokes	Surviving Childhood	The Ultimate Business Networking Guide	What Living on A Budget Taught Me
Confessions Over Wine	Believing in My Greatness	10 Signs I'm on the Right Path	Having Hope
Diary of a Street Cat	5 Songs to Cheer You Up	When I Was a Child	My Favourite Book

My Writing Dream	Overcoming Anxiety	Embracing Individuality	What It Means to Cry
Treasured Memories	Encouragement for Entrepreneurs	My Favourite Love Story	How to Run A Business

Feeling brave? Share your story in the *Writing With Confidence* Facebook group!

PART SIX:
ARTICLES ON WRITING

CONTENTS

WHY YOU SHOULD WRITE THAT BOOK

Are you that person who has always wanted to write a book, but hasn't taken that first step?

Perhaps you've made a start but got distracted and swayed away by your everyday responsibilities. Or maybe you have a great idea but you're worried nobody else will love it like you do.

You've been thinking about writing a book for years, even toyed with possible titles, perhaps discussed it with friends, and yet you haven't written a word.

If you're waiting for the right time in your life, perfect day, weather, conditions, environment, mood, and confidence before you finally put pen to paper, well I'm sorry, but you've been wasting time and it's time to stop.

You talk more about writing than actual writing, and therefore the book you have inside is still in your head. I know this sounds harsh but here it is, the cold, harsh truth: your writing is not your priority. Not yet, anyway. And all of that can change the minute you decided that this is more than a dream, it is a life goal that you can reach if you simply commit to making it part of your daily routine.

Your knowledge and expertise didn't come with ease, you spent time agonising over plot and scene choices, you've had the perfect ending in your head for months, and all that comes next is to get it onto paper or onto a word document.

This gorgeous idea, story, concept, whatever it is specifically, can only be birthed through your energy, your words, your action, so without any of that it just won't get written. It won't write itself, it needs you to believe in it and yourself enough to deliver the idea.

It is important for you to know that it won't write itself because it needs you to believe in it and yourself enough to deliver the idea.

Just in case you aren't entirely convinced, here are five reasons why I know that you should write that book:

Nobody can do it quite like you. There is nobody on this planet who can write about your experiences quite like you. You are unique, your perspective is going to be different and this is your selling point. This is what makes you stand out. And there are going to be a lot of people who love the way you construct your sentences, create believable characters and build a strong plot, and they are going to be the people who buy your book.

You've been putting it off for years. Honestly, if you don't do it now, when will you? It is not guaranteed that you will reach a time in your life when you have nothing but spare time on your hands with nothing to do. In fact, our lives are so busy at all stages, and we make time for what we consider important. I met a woman once who scheduled a daily alert in her phone to write a book, but she never sat down to write. She had it there, didn't remove it, but ignored it and continued with her day. But she still wanted to write a book.

My point is, that time will pass anyway, it's what you do with it that makes the difference. You don't have to write all of it in one sitting, you just have to make a start.

It will make a difference. Don't underestimate the power of the written word. I've written fiction about domestic violence and still been contacted by people who felt moved by it. Your story could be the very thing that stops somebody from giving up and inspires them to move forward. Your perspective could shed light on an area otherwise unknown. Your experience could shape the opinions of those who are looking to learn and eager to help. Your story could show someone else in the world that they aren't alone. Whether you stick to fiction or branch out into personal development, education or other areas, what you have to offer is going to be different from anyone else if you stay authentic, and that is what will appeal to readers.

It will open up opportunities you would never have imagined. There's something special about writing and publishing a book. When I wrote my first novel, I hadn't given much thought about what would happen beyond publishing. What happened was more than I could ever expect for myself, and it is what brings me here today writing this blog post for you. Being an author will open doors, windows, and opportunities to you, that will push you outside of your comfort zone.

You will be invited to speak and read at events, facilitate workshops, sell your books and collaborate with people and businesses who now find value in what you say. Amazing, right? And it sounds bizarre because it really is, but ultimately from the minute you begin to pour a little faith in yourself, the Universe responds with more of the same.

You will grow. I can only speak from experience on this one, both first-hand and being witness to it in others, but writing a book will be the making of you. Holding a book in your hands with your name on the cover and your words on the pages, that right there is phenomenal. It blows out all the negative self-talk and self-sabotaging ways out the water because you achieved something so big. You can't help but feel proud of yourself, even if you secretly worry about the feedback from others. Because no matter what they say, you're the one who believed in themselves enough to write a book.

I'm hoping I've done enough here to convince you that it's time to put pen to paper. I'll be thrilled to know that you've at least made notes, thought about scenes and created a strong character to drive your book forward. Or perhaps have the chapters of your self-help guide carefully planned out. Whatever your book, please don't delay.

Your readers are waiting.

HOW TO BE A WRITER

For the longest time, I didn't feel like an author. Even after I'd published four books, I felt very much a writer, and for me that was a separate thing altogether. Could I distinguish why? No, but I knew I felt the difference long before I had the vocabulary to verbalise it.

We're in an era of self-published authors and I know traditional literary authors may turn their nose up at that. I know that in amongst the flurry of books being published left, right and centre, the art of writing has been lost in favour for popularity.

For me, anyone can be an author. Anyone can put words together and make a story, upload it to the internet, pick their pre-made cover from their chosen self-publishing platform and then press 'publish'. Anyone can do it, it isn't hard and for that reason alone so many do it. And why wouldn't they? Being an author brings you many rewards, invitations to speak at events, deliver workshops, collaborate on projects, be interviewed on radio and much more. It's viewed as a point of success, and so it should be, but I feel like it has become so glamourised that the point of being an author has been lost.

Yes, I am an author too but I don't claim to be the best. I'm still working on it and that's okay. I'm a writer at core, and this means I have a love of the craft of writing too. However, I've given this some thought and have put together 5 basic points on how you can become a writer, or perhaps a better writer than you already are:

Write. Nobody wakes up one day and is the perfect writer ever. It is a skill, a muscle that needs to be exercised regularly to perform at its best. Don't wait for the moment of inspiration to arrive, sometimes we must push through what we feel and write anyway. It's necessary if we want to reach our word count, deadline or writing goals. I have met many people who say to me "I've always wanted to write a book" but are they writing anyway? Unlikely, because they have put barriers and blocks in front of them, and rather than write a little bit daily or a few times a week, they do nothing but hold onto the dream and take no action towards it.

Read. This may seem bizarre but reading helps you to write better. It helps to improve your own spelling and grammar, as well as how you structure your writing and the tone you use. Take note of the genres you enjoy the most, especially the way the author draws you in. Is this the type of genre you'd like to write in? Also, read books about writing by writers. Reading for pleasure is awesome, but even more amazing is to read for development.

Learn. As much as you read and write, your quest to become a better writer doesn't start and end with you. It's easy to assume that you can teach yourself everything, but it's okay to step forward with the guidance of trained professionals. Writing classes, YouTube tutorials and further education can all help you improve your craft. Academic writing is certainly very different from writing from yourself, but it adds so much value to the skills and knowledge you already possess. It demands our writing to be at a high level, we must push ourselves beyond what we know to understand and apply new techniques and skills. How can you be the best writer you can be, if you don't take the opportunities available to improve your craft?

Explore. Don't be a one trick pony, just don't do it. Over the years I've tried a mixture of writing articles about feminism and music, event reviews, poetry, short stories, books and more, and I am still discovering how I like to express myself. I enjoy the casualness of blogging, but also the respect and confidence that comes with writing books. To find out what you do best, you must try different types of writing. So, don't be afraid to try a different genre, a different type of writing. It's how we figure out what we're good at it.

Persevere. Writing isn't easy, not at all if you take it seriously. There are going to be days where you know you should write but can't face picking up a pen. You're going to have to persevere against the negative self-talk and self-doubt. It is likely you will convince yourself that your writing is dreadful and the world will hate it, yet still think about writing until your head hurts. Your desire to complete a written piece must be greater than your desire to give up.

Most of all, don't listen to the noise around you when you write. Let the words flow naturally, the style takes its own shape and the words leap off the page with a life of their own. Avoid drawing comparisons between yourself and other writers, because we all do things differently. It takes discipline to dedicate time to finding out exactly how you write, accepting your style and loving yourself for it.

The narrative doesn't need to be that all writers bathe with self-loathing, not for you anyway. You define how you write. You define your experience of being a writer. So, go and do exactly that.

THESE 9 MISTAKES WILL DESTROY YOUR WRITING.

I'm not a perfect writer and I don't know if I will ever be perfect. When I published my first book, I was more focused on the achievement of a life goal than of the quality of work it took to get me there. My books being well-written wasn't always a priority, but this has changed over time as I have seen the benefits of producing a piece of work I can be proud of. I think that if you invest your time in anything, it should give you an outcome you can be happy with.

With that in mind, I'd like to welcome you to some of the biggest mistakes you can make, and offer solutions on how you can avoid them. And this is beyond the obvious spelling and grammar errors, I want you to be mindful of a few other important points:

1. Comparison – It's easy to look at other writers and use their work as "proof" that your work is not up to standards. But there are two ways you can look at it. You can either use the magic of what someone else has written to cripple you or you can choose to be inspired by it and allow it to motivate you to do better. Don't stop writing because you don't consider yourself as good as Dorothy Koomson of Cecelia Ahern, instead use it to prompt you: what initially grabbed your attention? What did you like about it the most? How do they create believable characters? How did they keep you reading? And use your answers to guide you when you write.

2. Rushing – When we write a book, we are so eager to meet the finishing line and often become frustrated by how long the process takes. There is no overnight solution, it takes some time to create a masterpiece. When we rush, we leave out valuable information and our writing suffers from a lack of attention. We don't convey the message we intended to, instead our readers get a diluted version simply because you couldn't be bothered to explain it. Be bothered. Take your time. Don't focus on finishing the word count, focus instead on being satisfied with the quality.

3. Overuse of profanity – I must say, in everyday life, I have a potty-mouth and it's not uncommon for it to crop up in a blog or even in one of my books. But I believe we must be strategic in our use of swear words in our writing. Use it sparingly. Does it add value to the dialogue? Does it fit the profile of the character? Is it within context? Can you say what you need to without using it?

4. Overkill with capital letters – Have you ever read a whole paragraph of capital letters? It feels like someone is shouting at you, right? At least, that's how I read it because that is how grammar works. Think about making an impact without overkilling capital letters. The idea is that you encourage people to finish reading what you've written, not scare them off!

5. Lack of research – It makes sense to write what you know, right? Research can strengthen your writing, it adds credibility and positions you as an expert in that field. Even if you're writing fiction, it helps to do a little research so that your story is believable and makes sense to the readers.

6. Self-doubt – It's all well and good pursuing your writing goals, but be aware that you'll need a healthy dosage of self-belief to get you there. How can you make your daily word count if you've already decided you can't do it? How will you write that book if you've already told yourself that you'll fail? If you're reading this, that alone shows me you believe in yourself enough to read about writing, and perhaps it will take you a little further for you to try. Don't block yourself from your creativity. Tell yourself you will write today and make it happen. Don't worry about how good it is initially, just get the words written down!

7. Not reading at all – I love books and delved into the magical world of reading from a very young age. Over the years my preferred reading genres have changed, but the love of reading has stayed the same. At the time I write this, I've got a healthy pile of books to get through over summer. I noticed that my writing improved when I increased my reading. The structure of my writing changed and became more refined. The flow of my writing has improved, which enhances the readability for those who indulge in my work. If you don't read, your subconscious won't take in these subtle details and writing a book will seem a bit more of a challenge.

8. Not editing – Do I really need to go into this? Go beyond spellcheck. Top tip: Read it out loud, word for word, to see if it sounds right. If it doesn't, make some alterations. Plus, there are a world of editors available via the internet who can edit your work for a fee. This is well with the investment when you're writing a book.

9. Letting people's opinions shape your work – It's a huge deal to write anything, even more so to share it with the world. Your writing is going to prompt all sorts of reactions and some of it will be positive, others not so much. Constructive criticism is important, we need it to grow and improve our work. Often, people's perspective can offer us something we didn't even think about before, and we can use it to create an even better piece of writing. However, you don't have to take every single comment on board, not if you don't want to. Don't place yourself in the position of losing your style of writing, because that can't be taught. Not in the way you do it, anyway. So, take every suggestion with a pinch of salt, and apply whatever you feel will enhance your creativity.

I don't mind letting you know that I love what I've published so far but I'm not a big fan of the quality. In fact, this is why I don't promote my books as much as I should. I've finished my second year of a Creative & Professional Writing degree and it has opened my eyes. I've taken the time to read more, blogs and books alike, and to speak to people about writing. I've become a point of reference to those who are new on this journey and using the lessons I've gained I've helped them to avoid making the same mistakes. So, I hope you find the above information useful.

Tell me, what would you add to this list?

FIVE REASONS WHY YOU SHOULD START A BLOG

IT'S 2017 AND BLOGGING HAS BECOME INCREDIBLY POPULAR, BUT WHERE DOES THIS LEAVE YOU?

If you've been wondering if there's room for you to make your mark, then I am here to enlighten you. Why? Well, because the blogging world has yet to hear your perspective on a topic of your choice.

When I first began blogging, I didn't take it seriously, I'll be honest. Feel free to scroll through to my archives and find my early posts, and you'll see the huge difference between then and now. I'll go as far to say that I didn't make much of an effort and I didn't blog with any clear focus or plan. I just liked writing and that's what I did, but over the years my outlook has changed and I'm beginning to see what an asset a blog can be.

I approach this platform with a different mindset now and I'm hoping the little nuggets of wisdom I have will be enough to encourage you to do the same.

You'll find value in your own voice.

The awesome thing about blogging is that it gives you an opportunity to create an identity for yourself. Whether you write under your own name or opt for a pseudonym, the point is that either way this place becomes a focal point for where you find value in what you have to say. You become comfortable with your writing style, you begin to receive feedback from people you've never met but who love your writing. And that, that alone, gives you a confidence boost, plus confirms what you secretly knew all along: That you are destined for greatness.

It teaches you discipline.

It's not enough to blog once a month, you'll soon learn that to survive in the blogging community you need to be consistent, and regular. If you really care about your blog, you'll pay attention to the most popular posts and start t cover that area more and more to please your following. You'll learn to blog at least once a week, to promote often, and ultimately that the success of the blog depends on the actions you take daily. It sounds huge, and it can be if you don't plan ahead and post accordingly.

You'll gain experience and opportunities.

Similar to that of writing a book, a blog will open up doors and opportunities for you that you'll have never imagined. People get used to seeing you post and promote your content, you develop a reputation for being consistent in your niche, and before you know it you'll receive invites with all sorts of offers. Plus, as you become accustomed to blogging regularly, that extra experience will certainly have you picking up on trends much faster than when you did when you started out.

It will enhance your business.

Blogs are great for business. It offers an exclusive, sort of behind the scenes insight to what really goes down at headquarters. I treat my blog as an informal chat with my most loyal followers, sometimes sharing words of wisdom about life or tips about writing. I've used it to talk about my mental health, events I hold, my books, my coaching, all of which I then use to promote what I do. And that? Well, that brings me business, and all it cost me was half an hour of my time.

You'll make international connections.

What I love about writing on the internet, in general, is that you have no idea just who in the world is going to see it. It's easy to assume that all your friends and family are going to read your work, but usually, it's the people who are complete strangers who will love your posts and read every one. And that's okay. If it wasn't for the internet, we wouldn't the ability to reach people from all over the world with our words. I love that connection. It means my writing is travelling to places I haven't been to yet, and that can only lead to even greater opportunities.

Are you convinced? Let me know what you think via the Writing With Confidence Facebook group.

FOUR REASONS WHY YOUR WRITING IS RUBBISH.

It's likely you arrived at this part expecting to be inundated with insults and criticisms, all about how crap your writing is, and how I'm much better at it than you. Well, honey, I'm sorry to disappoint but this is not the day for that.

I understand how vulnerable we become when we share our writing with the world. We put ourselves in the firing line, or so it seems, and it is an uncomfortable feeling. Yet, when we do we allow the world to indulge in our written masterpieces and prove to ourselves that we can indeed achieve our goals. But it feels like a big leap. So, fear steps in and discourages us from even trying.

YOUR WRITING IS RUBBISH BECAUSE:

You told yourself it is. You affirmed it to yourself until it became a self-fulfilling prophecy. You expected rubbish writing and the universe delivered. You told yourself that nobody would read it because it's so horrible, and so you didn't bother putting it anywhere it could be found.

You gave up before you tried. You were so convinced that your writing was rubbish, that you didn't even bother finishing it. You had a great idea for a story but decided that your writing wasn't worthy enough to tell it.

You compared yourself to others and lost. You decided that there was no beginner's stage, in fact, you decided you can only start out as perfect. You decided that you must write as well as those who have written many books, you decided that you could only be as great as authors of bestsellers or not write at all.

You tell people it is rubbish. You've mentioned your writing to others but have added a negative comment to it. You paint a picture of mediocrity to people and so they come to expect only that.

Feel good? Of course, it doesn't, and that's the point. When you hold onto this belief, it won't make you feel good. It won't make you feel motivated to write, to finish what you've started or to try something new. It won't push you to reach your goal of writing a book because you've already decided that it isn't worth the effort. It won't inspire you to tell your story or to use your writing to bring light to a much-needed cause. You've already told yourself that there's no point.

But I think you're wrong.

Ultimately, you create your reality. You are in charge. Your mind believes the messages repeated to it constantly. If you believe your writing is rubbish, you reinforce it with your thoughts and actions. You put so much energy into that belief, that eventually it manifests. You know about the Law of Attraction, right?

You can only become great at anything if you choose to entertain the possibility of it happening. If you choose to try, you'll see how far you can get. If you find the positives in your writing, you'll give yourself enough confidence to address the areas you still need to learn. If you read about writing and attend writing events, it is likely you'll become part of a network you can learn from. If you speak highly of your work and the inspiration behind it, people will want to read it. If you believe that your writing is good, you'll only expect the best from yourself and you'll be motivated to reach that standard every time.

We all have doubts but this level of self-deprecation can be damaging to your self-esteem, which will only affect your desire to write in the first place. Being a confident writer doesn't happen overnight, it takes daily acts to get to a point where you feel good about yourself, and daily practice until your writing develops.

So, think about what you can do each day to challenge the negative thoughts you have about your writing. How can you become your own biggest fan? How can you dismiss this false idea of being a rubbish writer, and commit instead to something more positive? If affirmations are your thing, and you're not quite ready to acknowledge your current creative greatness, start with this: My writing is improving all the time and I am creating a masterpiece.

Now bring that mantra to life. Write with the expectation that you will produce something good, and it is likely that you will.

And when you do? Tell me all about it.

ON WRITING: PC OR PAPER?

I CONFESS: I'M A LOVER OF THE LAPTOP BUT A SOUL MATE OF PEN AND PAPER.

It's fair to say that most writers will have a preference of tools when it comes to creating their written masterpieces.

I've tried and tested the different methods over the years and although I love writing, I feel the creativity flows with ease when I put a pen to paper. I tend to plan on paper and write it up in 'best' on my laptop, both methods go hand in hand and it works beautifully.

But I was interested to know if other writers share the same preference or perhaps you could provide a better argument for writing purely onto an electrical device.

To assist you in your decision-making, I've thought about and made some valid points for you to consider:

<u>PAPER</u>

Raw creativity – That feeling of freedom as your pen glides over the paper, allowing your thoughts to run wild and ideas pour out onto the page.

It just flows – You're not worried about spelling mistakes or grammar, all that matters is that you write authentically and it will make sense later.

It feels magical – You're in the moment, you're embracing this creative buzz and once you start writing, you can't stop!

You can remember how you were feeling at the time you wrote it – There's an emotional connection. Those little doodles at the corners of the page and the random scribbles in the margin, all helps you take a trip back to the past to how you were feeling that day. When we're in the moment, everything can feel so intense, and this is reflected especially in our journal writing.

No pressure to be perfect – Spelling mistakes, grammar errors, structure faux pas, it's all fine when you're writing on paper. It's almost like you have accepted that perfection isn't required and the freedom a draft gives you is beautiful.

PC/LAPTOP/IPAD/ELECTRICAL DEVICE

It's more structured – The fact that you can mould the whole layout as you write is amazing. If you're writing poetry, it's easy to space down to another line. If you're writing articles, you can write in paragraphs and use templates to guide you (particularly in Google Docs).

You can check the spelling, grammar and word count, all with the click of a button – Once you've been staring at the screen for hours, you're able to use technology to help identify all the other areas that need attention. With the help of *Grammarly*, you can go one step further and make sure it all makes sense.

You can read what you wrote – Have you ever written something in a rush? Then can't read it back? Problems. More specifically, writer's problems. For the most part, you'll be able to read your own handwriting but when you type onto your laptop, there's no chance of you misreading what you've written, unless you aren't paying attention, of course.

You can edit as you write, without messing up your page – Exactly what it says on the tin. This is something I love about writing directly onto WordPress, is the fact that I can edit is as I go along. Sometimes what I'm writing turns out different to what I expected, when I come to edit I may add or remove features and that is easier to do with an electrical device. If blogs were handwritten, that would be a lot of starting over!

What works best for you? I'd love to know! Head on over to the *Writing With Confidence* Facebook group and share your preferences.

THE UGLY TRUTH ABOUT WRITING

PLACING VALUE IN YOUR CREATIVITY WON'T ALWAYS BRING YOU POSITIVE RESULTS, BUT YOU MUST PERSEVERE.

I've talked about the benefits of writing, which is important for anyone considering delving into their creativity. However, as with everything, there is another side of writing that I feel inclined to share.

I don't want to put you off or add to an existing worry you may already have. At the same time, I don't want to mislead you into thinking that writing is all sunshine and rainbows either. Writing can absolutely change your life, but you need to be ready for all aspects of the ride.

It's not easy. Sure, you can put pen to paper but when you begin writing for an audience the pen feels heavier. You start doubting your ideas, you compare yourself to the greats and feel inferior, and at times you stare at a blank screen waiting for inspiration to start. While you had the motivation to begin with, actually maintaining it becomes a challenge, and often when starting out we're just not quite prepared for it. But you can do it!

Not everybody will be a fan. You may write something that you love, put it on your blog or in your book, and receive positive feedback. And then there will be that one comment, that one negative review that has you doubting your whole existence. Remember, your writing style isn't going to appeal to everybody. The whole world isn't your target audience. And while you can take constructive criticism on board and use that when reflecting on your writing, don't allow it to define the work that you do.

It will push you outside of your comfort zone. You've written your first blog post, pressed 'publish' and now you're suddenly feeling vulnerable. Why? Well, writing for yourself is one thing, but actually sharing that with other people can feel scary. Owning your work in public takes great strength, and this is a challenge for many new writers as you'll be at a point where you're yet to find value in what you do. In the writing industry, you have to develop a thick skin and love your work fiercely, but not so much that you don't try new genres or new writing types. Embarking on a writing journey is a commitment to stepping outside of who you are now and moving closer to who you could be.

You'll often hate what you write but be compelled to continue. I'll be honest, it's rare that I love anything that I write in the moment that I write it. I've been inspired by pieces instantly, but the majority of the time I'm convinced it's awful. However, the desire to write is greater than that so I persevere and eventually I produce a good piece of work. You're not going to love what you write straight away. You'll be so anxious about what other people might think, that you'll start creating negative opinions before anyone else has a chance to. This is normal, but pushing past this to write anyway is what makes you a writer.

Despite all of this, I urge you to write anyway. You'll be so glad you did.

WRITE WHERE YOU CAN

So, you've had an amazing idea for a book or blog, and you're ready to get started on it, only you don't know where you can make the time to write. Now what?

How frustrating it can be for life to get in the way of our writing plans, for our weekends to pass us by without an afternoon of spare time we can invest in our creativity. Or perhaps that free afternoon arrives and you just don't feel like it. The inspiration to write was whispering in your ear when you were at work, but now you're at home you just want to relax and enjoy doing nothing. Perhaps you find those few hours you could write in peace, but your pen runs out of ink or the phone rings and before you know it you're just not in the mood.

I get it, I really do. This used to be me. It often still is. Still waiting for the perfect day, time, atmosphere, temperature, all sorts of qualifying conditions I tell myself I need before I think about putting pen to paper. But it's all bullshit. Yeah, I said it.

The reality is this: **we make time for whatever and whoever is important to us.** If writing a book is important to you, you'll find the time in your schedule to make it happen. You'll prioritise it over less urgent tasks because it is vital for you to reach that goal.

Are you the kind of person who talks more about writing than actually writing anything? Are you spending time hyping yourself up rather than building something to be hyped about? Have you spent more time planning your book than writing the chapters?

It's time to stop the procrastination, honey. And yes, I know you know what I'm talking about.

We procrastinate when things feel hard. Once you've planned your book, part of you is so overwhelmed that you begin to wonder if you can actually manage to pull it off. Before you've even started, it feels like a huge mountain to climb and suddenly typing away at your laptop doesn't seem as fun as it once did. Perhaps your deadlines are ambitious but don't consider your daily roles and responsibilities. Or maybe you're waiting for the "right time" to get started but as it didn't arrive you're happy to wait until the following week.

Stop. It. Now.

I get it. Writing is hard, it is, but it doesn't have to be. Stop hiding from your dreams, your ideas, your goals and the potential greatness you're flirting with. Stop talking yourself out of a creative venture that you haven't even tried yet. Stop telling yourself that you can't do it, that it's impossible, that it's hard. Stop telling yourself that it can only happen at 1pm on Saturdays if you're in a good mood, stop telling yourself that you need to be in a good mood to make it happen. Stop telling yourself that you need all the followers, the likes, the comments, the shares, the social media recognition before you start writing that book. Stop it right now.

Procrastination can creep in through all sorts of cracks, no matter how focused or determined you are. But don't let it win.

Sometimes the biggest barrier between us and the book we want to write is ourselves. My fifth book (this book) should have been published in early 2017. It's scheduled for release in August 2017. Why did I leave it so long?

Part of me was worried that it was terrible and that nobody will read it. Another part of me wondered if it was good enough at all and if I should have focused on writing my second novel instead. But another part of me needs to acknowledge what an achievement it is to have written a book (again) and allow myself to share it with the world. The idea was mine, sure, but the intention was never to keep it to myself. Isn't that why we write anyway?

This article isn't intended to guilt you into writing, but to prompt you to think about where you're really spending your time. If writing is important to you, whether you're writing a book or a journal, you will make time for it.

It can be ten minutes every morning before you get out of bed.

It can be ten minutes every evening before you go to sleep.

It can be ten minutes while you wait for your bath to fill.

It can be ten minutes while you wait to see your doctor.

It can be ten minutes while you wait for the dryer to finish its cycle.

It can be ten minutes while your children play in the garden.

It can be ten minutes of your 30-minute bus journey.

Or ten minutes of your lunch break.

Maybe even ten minutes in the morning while you enjoy that first cup of coffee.

You have ten minutes, right? We all do. These moments of opportunity to write often pass us because we're not looking for them. But I'm encouraging you to seek them out, identify where in your day you have 10 minutes to write and take full advantage of it. And you really don't need to write a full chapter, nor do you need your notes to utilise those 10 minutes.

You can write on a scrap of paper.

You can write using the memo pad on your phone.

You can voice record your ideas.

You can make notes of ideas.

You can brainstorm topics.

You can write poetry.

You can write.

Literally, write what you can and where you can. Although ten minutes a day doesn't seem like much, those little steps you take will add up. Those few minutes dedicated to your writing will have the creativity pouring out of you. And isn't that the point?

Try it. Let me know how you get on.

ABOUT THE AUTHOR

Annika Spalding is an award-winning author, a writing coach and workshop facilitator. Her books Shattered Dreams (2013), The Soaring Butterfly (2014), Reflections (2015), Shine (2015) and Get Back On Track With Self-Love (2017) are all self-published and are available on Amazon.

Annika used her love of stories to escape the trauma of her childhood and has indulged in writing ever since. Her writing has featured on online publications such as The F Word UK blog and The Voice Online, as well as printed literature at the Fawcett Society and others. Annika has contributed to company newsletters and co-created a newsletter for parents in women's refuges. True to form, wherever she is, Annika has always found a way to incorporate writing into her work.

In September 2015, Annika enrolled on a Creative and Professional Writing degree at the University of Wolverhampton and hasn't looked book since.

Featuring on BBC WM, Switch Radio and Newstyle Radio, Annika has become a recognisable and reputable brand known for creativity and empowerment.

In October 2016, Annika was awarded Author of Colour at BEXLive, cementing the recognition of her work by the community.

Annika launched her coaching business in early 2017, working 1:1 with people who are ready to write their books. Details of this can be found at www.writingwithconfidence.co.uk

Annika blogs about writing, mental health and empowerment over at her blog: www.annikaspalding.com

Annika lives a fabulous life, in Sandwell, UK, with her two children and a fridge full of wine.

66732629R00058

Made in the USA
Lexington, KY
22 August 2017